S0-BOM-392

¼/04

Factual Adviser
Dr. Mari Williams
Research Officer, Business History Unit
London School of Economics
London

Series Editor: Nicole Lagneau
Book Editor: Maria Ropek
Teacher Panel: Maureen Burns, David Caine, Cathy Loxton
Designer: Ewing Paddock
Production: Rosemary Bishop
Picture Research: Diana Morris

Adapted and first published in
the United States in 1989 by
Hampstead Press, 387 Park Ave.
South, New York, NY 10016
All rights reserved

Printed and bound in Belgium by
Proost International Book Production

Library of Congress Cataloging-in-Publication Data

Stott, Carole.
　Into the unknown/Carole Stott.
　　p.　cm. — (Women history makers)
　Bibliography: p.
　Includes index.
　Summary: Examines how astronomer Caroline Herschel,
aviator Amy Johnson, and astronaut Sally Ride made significant
contributions in the work of their choice despite male prejudice.
　ISBN 0-531-19513-9
　1. Herschel, Caroline Lucretia, 1750–1848—Juvenile literature.
2. Johnson, Amy—Juvenile literature.　3. Ride, Sally—Juvenile
literature.　4. Women astronomers—Germany—Biography—Juvenile
literature.　5. Women air pilots—Great Britain—Biography—Juvenile
literature.　6. Women astronauts—United States—Biography—Juvenile
literature.　7. Astronomers—Germany—Biography—Juvenile
literature.　8. Air pilots—Great Britain—Biography—Juvenile literature.
　9. Astronauts—United States—Biography—Juvenile literature.
[1. Herschel, Caroline Lucretia, 1750–1848.
2. Johnson, Amy.　3. Ride, Sally.　4. Women astronomers.　5. Woman
air pilots.　6. Women astronauts.　7. Astronomers.　8. Air pilots.
　9. Astronauts.]　I. Title.　II. Series.
QB36.H58S86 1989
500.5′092′2—dc19　　　　　　　　　　　　88–25921
[B]　　　　　　　　　　　　　　　　　　　　　　CIP
[920]　　　　　　　　　　　　　　　　　　　　　AC

Acknowledgments
We would like to thank John Murray Publishers Ltd for their kind permission to quote from *Memoirs and Correspondence of Caroline Herschel* by Mrs. John Herschel, 1876; Unwin Hyman Ltd for permission to quote from *First Flight, The Untold Story of the Wright Brothers* by John Evangelist Walsh, 1975; the Royal Astronomical Society for permission to quote from *The Scientific Papers of Sir William Herschel . . .*, collected and edited by the Royal Society and the Royal Astronomical Society, with a biographical introduction by J. L. E. Dreyer, 1912; Time Life International Ltd for permission to quote from *Women Aloft* by Valerie Noolman, 1981; Collins Publishers for permission to quote from *Amy Johnson* by Constance Babington Smith, 1967; The British Interplanetary Society for permission to quote from *Journal of the British Interplanetary Society*, 1987; the University of Pennsylvania for permission to quote from *ISIS*, 1987; the Sky Publishing Corporation for permission to quote from *Sky and Telescope*, 1987; Cambridge University Press for permission to quote from *The Herschel Chronicle*, edited by Constance A. Lubbock, 1933; and Michael Joseph Ltd for permission to quote from *First on the Moon, A Voyage with Neil Armstrong, Michael Collins, Edwin E. Aldrin Jr.* by Gene Farmer and Dora Jane Hamblin, 1970.

We acknowledge the source of quotes from the following: *The Los Angeles Times* 5/13/1982; *Current Biography* journal, 1983; *The Washington Times* 6/14/1983; *The Washington Post* 5/9/1983; *A Salute to Women in Aerospace* by Lillian D. Kozloski, an unpublished compilation; and *The New York Times* 6/25/1983. We would like to thank those writers and publishers whom we have not been able to contact and whose work is reprinted in this publication. We invite them to contact us.

Cover captions:
Left: Caroline Herschel (1750–1848) and her brother observing the skies (see pages 10–19).
Top right: Sally Ride (b. 1951) (see pages 30–41).
Bottom right: Amy Johnson (1903–1941) (see pages 20–29).
Back cover: Wright brothers flying, 1908 (see page 20).
Title page caption: astronaut working in space.

INTO THE UNKNOWN

Carole Stott

Hampstead Press New York 1989

About this book

Half the people in the world are women. So why do women appear so seldom in books on history? One reason is that until recently, history has been mainly about public events; in the past, many people thought that women should not take part in these. But, all the same, some women defied what people thought and worked to change society for the better. Their public achievements made history or would have if historians had remembered to take notice of them.

In the past, many historians have shared the traditional view that a woman's real place was at home, serving her family. If they found proof to the contrary, they often didn't recognize it, or ignored it. (The only women they could never ignore were female rulers.) Often, too, they summed up women's achievements in a couple of sentences, or a footnote in small print. The books in this series aim to put the women history-makers back where they belong: in the world they helped change, and in the way that we remember that world.

The three women you will read about here belonged to the world of the late 18th and early 19th centuries, and the 20th century. The first, Caroline Herschel, originally came from Germany but found fame while living and working in Britain. The second, Amy Johnson, was British. The third, Sally Ride, is American. This book shows you what they have in common.

How to use this book

When studying the past, historians try to go back to what the people of the past actually wrote and said. In the sections of this book marked "**Witness**," you can read some of the things said by people living at the time of Caroline Herschel, Amy Johnson and Sally Ride, and comments from the women themselves. Keep a look-out for these.

When Amy Johnson set off from England in May 1930 to fly solo to Australia, she didn't really know what to expect. She was a qualified pilot and engineer, qualifications which were extremely rare among women, but she had no long-distance flying experience. The success of her trip made her world-famous and showed that women as well as men could make aviation history.

Contents

Women and history

Throughout history, men and women of courage have been willing to work in unexplored areas to make discoveries for themselves and others. Nobody who works in this way knows what exciting new discoveries they will make or what rewards or disappointments they will find. But many people prefer to be told about new subjects and new lands before they become involved in them or go to look for themselves. They prefer to keep to what they know and leave the exploration of the unknown to other people. Working in an unknown subject or traveling into an unknown area takes great courage and determination.

Work in the unknown can include making new discoveries, carrying out scientific investigations, traveling into unknown lands to meet unknown races, traveling by a new means of transportation, or leaving Earth altogether and journeying into the vast wastelands of unknown space. Two hundred years ago, women were not as involved in this type of work as they are now. They were then expected to take a role that was secondary to men's. In general, the men were the workers while the women stayed at home to look after the house and children. It was expected that the men would work in the "unknown" areas.

There were, however, some women whose imagination was aroused by such work and who had the determination to become involved. Caroline Herschel, the first woman in this book, became a very talented astronomer. She was working in the 18th and 19th centuries, when the scientific world was almost exclusively male. There was no room for women; no one expected them to be interested in such subjects. Women like Caroline Herschel showed that they were interested, and proved that they had much to offer.

The expectations for women and of women improved slowly over the next 150 years. When Amy Johnson became involved in the 1930s in another area of the unknown, aviation, she experienced prejudice against her because she was female. Her achievements, and those of other women at that time, did much towards helping to give women equal opportunities. Increasing numbers of women wanted to have a choice in what they did and the same right to do something as men. The third woman, Sally Ride, an astronaut, benefited from the struggle for equality by women. Her employer gave equal opportunities to men and women. However, the public has made much of the fact that she is a woman in what is still regarded by some people as a man's world.

These three women have all made a significant contribution to the work area of their choice. Each of their situations has been different, where different social attitudes have prevailed according to the time and the stage of development of the subject they were working in. Each of them in their own way has explored into the unknown.

Caroline Herschel, 1750–1848, was born in Hanover, Germany. She moved to England in 1772 and became a very dedicated astronomer, observing night after night. She became famous, received many awards and gained the respect of the male-dominated astronomical community for her work.

Below, Sally Ride was born in 1951 in California. She trained as a physicist at Stanford University and then as an astronaut for NASA's space program. In June 1983, she became the first American woman to fly in space. In spite of earlier campaigns, women had not been allowed to train as astronauts. Sally Ride's flight marked for all women a great moment in the American space program.

Above, Amy Johnson, 1903–1943, was born into a middle-class family in northern England. In her early twenties she took up flying and earned her pilot's and engineer's licenses. Her solo and long-distance flying achievements brought her fame and gained respect for all women aviators in what had once been regarded as a man's world.

A new planet

Caroline Herschel and her brother William were moving again. Their last house in Bath had proved inconvenient because it had no garden space for their telescopes and they found it a nuisance to observe with them in the street. Caroline was supervising the removal of the household goods and instruments while William had gone ahead to arrange the telescopes in the garden of the new house. He did not want to lose a night from his regular program of observing the stars in the heavens. The first telescope he set up was the one which was seven feet long. That first evening, March 13, 1781, while Caroline Herschel was busy with household chores, William Herschel looked through the telescope and noticed "a curious either nebulous star or perhaps a comet." He did not know it then but he had discovered a new planet, Uranus.

Ever since humankind has looked up at the sky, people have known of the existence of planets other than Earth: of Mercury, Venus, Mars, Jupiter and Saturn. Astronomers in the 18th century were convinced these were all the planets in the solar system, the family of planets that moves around our local star, the Sun.

When William Herschel looked into the sky that night and saw something unusual, he did not think it could be a planet. In all of recorded history, no new major member of the solar system had been discovered. Perhaps the fuzzy patch he saw was a comet, an occasional visitor to the solar system, or perhaps it was a nebula, a much more distant object, way beyond our solar system.

When it was proved soon afterwards that this object could be a new planet, it marked a great change in the life of the Herschels, and as this news became accepted during the course of 1781, it affected the thinking of all astronomers. Uranus was so far away that overnight the solar system doubled in size. Astronomers throughout Europe had to rethink many of their ideas. Many of them wanted to know where to observe the planet. They also wanted to meet its discoverer William and his sister, Caroline Herschel, who assisted him.

William Herschel was soon to meet the King, George III, who had a very keen interest in astronomy and had his own observatory at Kew, just outside London. In 1782, William Herschel wrote to his sister, "I have had an audience of His Majesty this morning and met with a very gracious reception. I presented him with a drawing of the solar system, and had the honor of explaining it to him and the Queen." For a short time, the new planet was even known as *Georgium Sidus*

Left, these Parisians of 1811 are looking at something unusual in the sky, a comet. The artist who drew this picture has made the comet look brighter in the sky than it really was. Comets can be very difficult to see and it takes a specialized astronomer like Caroline Herschel to discover them.

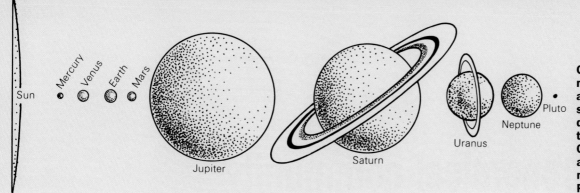

Our solar system consists of nine planets which revolve around the Sun. They are shown here in their order of distance from the Sun and in their relative sizes. When Caroline Herschel was working as an astronomer, people did not know about Neptune and Pluto.

(George's Star) in appreciation of the King's interest in William Herschel. The Herschels moved to Datchet to be near George III in Windsor. William Herschel became a professional and full-time astronomer when he took up the post of Astronomer to the King. William was awarded $400 a year and Caroline, his valuable assistant, was later given $100 a year.

Caroline Herschel had been brought to England by her brother. For the first 22 years of her life, she had kept house for her family. She said it was "my lot to be the Cinderella of the family (being the only girl)" and she could never find time for improving herself. In the 18th century, this was the role young women were expected

Below, astronomy was a popular interest in the 18th century. Some people would look at the sky and observe the changing patterns. Others preferred to read about astronomy and to learn from models, like the one here. This orrery shows how the planets in our solar system revolve around our local star, the Sun.

to assume. The sons in a family would go out to work, while the daughters looked after the house. If a girl did not have a husband to provide for her as she grew older, the responsibility would often be taken on by a brother.

William Herschel now acted as guardian to Caroline. She looked after the household affairs, leaving William free to pursue his interest in astronomy. She herself became interested in the subject and acted as assistant to her brother until she became an astronomer in her own right. When she moved to Datchet, at first she regretted leaving behind her singing career in Bath, but the subject of astronomy was soon to become a passion for her. Like William Herschel, she was to receive fame and honors for her astronomical work. This was most unusual in her time. The world of science was a man's world, and although there were a few women scientists in the late 18th and early 19th centuries, it was rare to see their work recognized.

"WITNESS

"I found I was to be trained for an assistant-astronomer, and by way of encouragement a telescope adapted for 'sweeping' consisting of a tube with two glasses, such as are commonly used in a 'finder,' was given me. I was 'to sweep for comets' and I see by my journal that I began August 22nd, 1782, to write down and describe all remarkable appearances I saw in my 'sweeps,' which were horizontal. But it was not till the last two months of the same year that I felt the least encouragement to spend the star-light nights on a grass-plot covered with dew or hoar frost, without a human being near enough to be within call."
Source: Caroline Herschel in her eighties. Quoted by Mrs. John Herschel, *Memoirs and Correspondence of Caroline Herschel*, 1876.

The astronomical community

When William Herschel wanted to announce his discovery of the planet Uranus, he first notified the Bath Philosophical Society and then the news was forwarded to the Royal Society in London. The Royal Society, founded in 1662, was one of a number of academies of science that had been established in Europe in the 17th century. The French one was founded in 1666, and the Berlin Academy in 1700. There, groups of men of science would meet and discuss the scientific problems of the day. New discoveries such as Herschel's would be reported at one of the regular meetings, and an account would be published in the Society's journal. Many of the astronomers that were Fellows of the Royal Society worked for a university or a major observatory.

William Herschel entered a scientific community that was dominated by men, but this was not surprising to him. Women were excluded from studying and working at universities and so they were automatically barred from the scientific academies when they were formed. Although the societies in London, Paris and Berlin did not have a regulation excluding women, none of the societies admitted them. It was not until halfway through the 20th century that women were accepted at these three societies. Women had only been accepted at some European universities in the very late years of the 19th century. But it did not mean that there were no women working in science, and in particular in astronomy. A few women were working in private observatories. Their role was that of assistant to the male astronomer, although they would do just as much work, and do it as well, as the man. As in family life,

Few women became involved in astronomy in the late 18th and early 19th centuries. In Britain, two women, Caroline Herschel and Mary Somerville (above), her junior by thirty years, were acknowledged for their astronomical work.

Below, the leading people in science of the early 19th century are gathered together at the Royal Institution, a center of scientific learning in London. William Herschel is on the left, next to the globes.

In the Octagon Room of the Royal Observatory at Greenwich, astronomers make observations with their telescopes. Some astronomers were paid to work in specially designed observatories like this. The amateur astronomers had to provide their own instruments and usually worked at home.

CAMERAM STELLATAM.

the woman's role was seen as a support to the man earning the money.

One woman working in astronomy at the beginning of the 18th century was Maria Winkelmann. She worked alongside her husband, Gottfried Kirch, at the Academy of Sciences in Berlin. She was his recognized but unofficial assistant. Yet she shared the workload of calculations, observations and calendar-making. When she discovered a comet, Kirch's name was put on the report of the discovery, as he was the Academy Astronomer and this was the first scientific achievement of the young Academy.

When her husband died, Maria Winkelmann applied to become Academy Astronomer. Although she was among the leading astronomers of the country, she did not have a university degree and was not considered a serious candidate. The Berlin Academy was also concerned about what effect the hiring of a woman would have on its reputation. She took her case to the King, but after one and a half years of active petitioning, she was finally rejected. The reasons for her rejection were never spelled out but she felt her misfortunes were due to her sex. She continued to argue that a woman can become as "skilled as a man at observing and understanding the skies."

Caroline Herschel also started her astronomical career as assistant to a man, her brother William. She became increasingly involved in his work, noting down his observations for him, calculating positions for him, helping him to make telescopes and finally having her own telescope and her own observing program. She knew the value of a good assistant, and wrote that an observer using a telescope to survey the sky "wants nothing but a being who can and will execute his commands . . ." She willingly spent her time assisting her brother up until the time of his marriage.

When William Herschel married, Caroline became free to concentrate on her own astronomy. In 1835, she was granted Honorary Membership of the recently founded Royal Astronomical Society, the astronomers' learned society. This was for the invaluable and unceasing assistance she gave to her brother and for her own program of observations and calculations. She was one of the first women in Europe to receive an award for her astronomical work.

WITNESS

"There is [in Berlin] a most learned woman who could pass as a rarity. Her achievement is . . . in the most profound doctrines of astronomy . . . She favors the Copernican system (the idea that the sun is at rest) like all the learned astronomers of our time . . . she knows how to handle marvelously the quadrant and the telescope . . ."
Source: written by Leibniz about Maria Winkelmann, 1709. Quoted by Londa Schiebinger, "Maria Winkelman at the Berlin Academy. A Turning Point for Women in Science," *ISIS*, 1987.

"That she be kept on in an official capacity to work on the calendar or to continue with observations simply will not do. Already during her husband's lifetime the society was burdened with ridicule because its calendar was prepared by a woman. If she were now to be kept on in such a capacity, mouths would gape even wider."
Source: Jablonski writing to Leibniz, 1710, about Maria Winkelmann. Quoted in same journal as above.

"Age has not abated my zeal for the emancipation of my sex from the unreasonable prejudice in Britain against literary and scientific education for women."
Source: Mary Somerville, in the 1860s. Quoted by Kenneth Weitzenhoffer in "The Education of Mary Somerville," *Sky and Telescope*, 1987.

Seeing into space

The very first time that the telescope was turned upward to look at the sky, astronomers realized what a useful tool it was. The first person to use the newly invented telescope in this way was Galileo Galilei, in 1609. Up to then, astronomers had only their eyes for looking at the night sky. But now, as Galileo found, the telescope revealed new splendors in the heavens. Through it, astronomers could see mountains on the Moon which made them think that it could be a similar place to the Earth. They could see that the planet Jupiter had four moons traveling around it, just as our Moon travels around the Earth. The telescope could also see much further into space. It showed that there were many more stars in space than those that people could see with their eyes.

The telescope was useful to astronomers because it gave a better view of the heavenly objects they could see with their eyes, and revealed others that were previously beyond their vision. The telescope, by means of a lens or mirror, collected light from the distant object. The light then formed into an image of that object in front of the eyepiece of the telescope. The astronomer looked into the eyepiece to see the image of the distant object. The success of the telescope in allowing astronomers to see further into space depended on the amount of light that it collected, and the magnifying power of the eyepiece.

The earliest telescopes used lenses and were called refracting telescopes. The other main type of telescope, the reflecting telescope, which uses mirrors to reflect the light from the object to the observer's eye, came later. If an astronomer wanted a telescope he or she would either make it or instruct someone else to make it, specifying the type and size. If a certain type of telescope was needed for a particular job, the astronomer was likely to make it. When William Herschel wanted to see further and further into space, he built larger and larger telescopes that would collect more light and show even more. The best telescope for this type of job was a reflector. William Herschel would grind and polish the mirrors, assisted by his sister and brother, Caroline and Alexander.

At times, their home was transformed into a workshop. Alexander would be in one room making the wooden stands while Caroline and William produced the more important parts, the mirrors. William was in charge of the workshop and Caroline became a skilled worker. She underplayed her talents when she said, "I became in time as useful a member of the workshop as a boy might be to his master in the first year of his apprenticeship. . . ." Caroline was much more useful than a young boy just starting to learn telescope-making skills. She worked on a number of telescopes produced in the Herschel workshop and did the final work on a special telescope made for a great family friend, Sir William Watson.

On some evenings, Caroline Herschel used her brother's large telescope but as she was engaged in sweeping, or systematically searching, the sky for comets, she needed a telescope designed for this purpose. Her first one was "a tube with two glasses" (lenses) which had been given to her and adapted for her use. In time, she owned more powerful comet sweepers made especially for her by William Herschel.

When Caroline and William Herschel needed telescopes for observing, they made them themselves. Others were not as talented; these two gentlemen in their private observatory bought their instruments.

 **WITNESS**

". . . I was much hindered in my musical practice by my help being continually wanted in the execution of the various contrivances, and I had to amuse myself with making the tube of pasteboard for the glasses which were to arrive from London, for at that time no optician had settled at Bath."
Source: Caroline Herschel recalling how she first became involved in making telescopes. Quoted by Mrs. John Herschel, *Memoirs and Correspondence of Caroline Herschel*, 1876.

"Many visitors had the curiosity to walk through it, among the rest King George III, and the Archbishop of Canterbury, following the King, and finding it difficult to proceed, the King turned to give him the hand, saying, 'Come my Lord Bishop, I will show you the way to Heaven!'"
Source: Caroline Herschel passing on an anecdote about William Herschel's 40-foot telescope, which she also used, to her nephew's wife. Quoted in same book as above. See picture on page 19.

The Astronomer Royal, Nevil Maskelyne, remarked in 1793, "I paid Dr. and Miss Herschel a visit 7 weeks ago. She showed me her 5 foot Newtonian telescope made for her by her brother for sweeping the heavens . . . being designed to show objects very bright, for the better discovering any new visitor to our system that is Comets, or any undiscovered nebulae. It is a very powerful instrument, and shows objects very well." However good the telescope, the astronomer using it had to be able to recognize what he or she was looking at. The same distinguished astronomer went on to pay tribute to Caroline Herschel's observing ability, saying that ". . . whenever she sweeps in fine weather nothing can escape her."

Brilliant discoveries

In her observing book, Caroline Herschel wrote on August 1, 1786, "I have counted one hundred nebulae today, and this evening I saw an object which I believe will prove tomorrow night to be a comet." But, to her disappointment, it rained throughout the following day and the prospects for observing that evening were not good. However, at 1 am on the following morning, the weather did clear up a little and she was able to write in her book, "The object of last night is a comet." With these words, she recorded the discovery of her first comet. She was to go on to discover seven more in the years that followed. This was a feat unrivaled by any other astronomer and one that secured her name in history.

Caroline Herschel had not expected to become a famous astronomer when she first came to England in 1772. She was leaving a very dreary and domesticated life behind in Hanover where she had looked after her aged parents and brothers. When he brought her to England, her kind-hearted brother William was giving her the chance to develop her own interests and to enrich her life. The interests she did follow, however, were William's. She was so grateful to him for making her life more interesting that she first became involved in music and then astronomy so that she could assist William in his pursuits.

In the 18th century, when men provided financial security at home, women were expected to be supportive and Caroline Herschel accepted this role. It was only when William married and she was not needed to support him any more that Caroline was totally free to follow her own interests. By the time this happened in 1788, Caroline Herschel was well known for her astronomical work which she had grown to love. She was acknowledged as a skilled observer by European astronomers and received much praise from them, and distinctions from their Societies.

The French astronomer Alexandre Aubert wrote to her as soon as he had seen the first comet she had discovered. He said, "You have immortalized your name, and you deserve such a reward from the Being who has ordered all these things to move as we find them, for your assiduity in the business of astronomy . . ." Professor Encke, who also studied the comets, wrote some years later, to pay his respects to Caroline Herschel. He referred to her as a woman ". . . whose name is so intimately connected with the most brilliant astronomical discoveries of the age . . ."

Caroline Herschel was a very talented and hardworking astronomer. She was introduced to the subject by her brother. She went on to discover eight comets and had her star catalogs published. She observed the heavens night after night until well into old age.

For Caroline Herschel had not only discovered eight comets but had detected several remarkable nebulae and clusters of stars. She was also to have two star catalogs published by the Royal Society, and to be awarded the Gold Medal of the Royal Astronomical Society in 1828 for her work on the list of star clusters and nebulae observed by her brother William. In 1835, she was awarded Honorary Membership of the Royal Astronomical Society. Although this learned society had no women members, it acknowledged the role of women astronomers by bestowing this honor on two women at the same time: Mary Somerville, for her work in popularizing important scientific books of the period, and Caroline Herschel, who was by then in her eighties. It was an extraordinary distinction.

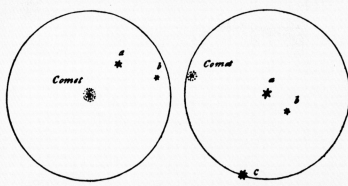

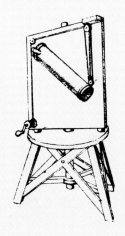

Right, a sketch of the telescope made for Caroline Herschel for searching for comets. She looked through the tube which moved up and down, and swung around on the stool-like base. The comets moved against the fixed background of the stars, as her drawings show (left).

WITNESS

"I am nothing, I have done nothing; all I am, all I know, I owe to my brother. I am only the tool which he shaped to his use — a well-trained puppy dog would have done as much."
Source: Caroline Herschel's typically modest comment, quoted by Mrs. John Herschel, *Memoirs and Correspondence of Caroline Herschel,* 1876.

"But the premium of the King of Denmark's medal, for the discovery of telescopic comets, provokes me beyond all endurance, for it is of no use to me. One of my eyes is nearly dark, and I can hardly find the line again I have just been tracing by feeling on paper."
Source: Caroline Herschel expressing her frustration at her failing sight, 1832, after receiving a medal. Quoted in same book as above.

As William Herschel kept his eye to the heavens, Caroline Herschel, acting as assistant, would write down his observations as he called them out to her. Sometimes she would sit in a bedroom window nearby, where she could hear William's instructions.

CAROLINE HERSCHEL

In the public eye

When the Royal Astronomical Society bestowed on Caroline Herschel their Honorary Membership, they stated that women astronomers should now be judged in the same way as men. They said that they should receive awards for the astronomical work they had done and not be treated differently because they were women. This is a judgment we would expect now, but this was not so in the time of Caroline Herschel. Women were treated differently: they could not study at universities, they had to work mostly as assistants and not full astronomers, and they were not allowed to join the learned societies and to meet openly with the scientists of the day.

The Royal Astronomical Society said that the sex of a woman astronomer "should no longer be an obstacle to her receiving any acknowledgment which might be held due." However, in practice, Caroline Herschel was to be an Honorary and not a full member of the Society, and as a woman she could not attend Society meetings. The attitudes of the country at large where women were playing a secondary role were still

More than one hundred years after Caroline Herschel started work as an astronomer, women were still usually assistant astronomers. Here, a group of American women assistants who did very important work on the classification of stars pose with the Director, E. C. Pickering, at Harvard College Observatory, 1913.

BIOGRAPHY

1750 Born March 16, Caroline Lucretia Herschel, in Hanover, Germany. Her father is an oboist with the Hanoverian Foot Guards; her mother manages household affairs.
1767 Death of Caroline Herschel's father. Caroline looks after the family.
1772 Her brother William brings her to Bath, England, to have a better life with him.
1781 William Herschel discovers the planet Uranus.
1782 Caroline moves with William to a new house near the King at Windsor Castle.
1783 Discovers three nebulae.
1786–1797 Discovers eight comets.
1787 Granted $100 a year by King George III to assist her brother.
1788 Her brother marries and so Caroline no longer has to keep house for him.

1798 Her star catalogs published by the Royal Society.
1822 Returns to Hanover.
1828 Receives the Gold Medal of the Royal Astronomical Society.
1832 Awarded a medal by the King of Denmark for her discoveries.
1835 Awarded Honorary membership of the Royal Astronomical Society.
1838 Royal Irish Academy elects her an honorary member.
1846 Awarded gold medal for science by the King of Prussia.
1848 January 9, dies in Hanover, aged 97.

influencing these men of science even though they claimed to be free of any prejudice.

In every other sense, the astronomical community consistently valued Caroline Herschel's work. They saw her talents as two-fold. She had helped her brother "to obtain his imperishable name," and the Royal Astronomical Society praised her "as an original observer [who] demands . . . our unfeigned thanks."

Caroline Herschel was by now very elderly and living out her final years in Hanover. Her interest in astronomy did not cease and according to her nephew's wife, ". . . no man of any scientific eminence passed through Hanover without visiting her." Yet her old age was to frustrate her. She wrote that "The few, few stars that I can get at out of my window only cause me vexation, for to look for the small ones of the globe, my eyes will not serve me any longer."

When accepting the Honorary Membership, she wrote to London that her "only regret [was] that at the feeble age of 85 I have no hope of making myself deserving of the great honor of seeing my name joined with that of the much distinguished Mrs. Somerville." As a result of her modesty and the current social values, she constantly underplayed the importance of her work.

She was always willing to be of assistance, and did not wish to trouble others with her astronomical work.

After her death, the President of the Royal Astronomical Society said that her memory would live "on its own merits, even though . . . the time should come when the astronomical celebrity of a woman will not, by the mere circumstance of sex, be sufficient to excite the slightest remark." However, it was nearly 70 years before the Society opened its doors to women and men on the same terms.

When Caroline and William Herschel lived near Windsor, William Herschel built a very large telescope which had a 40-foot long tube. For some years, it was the largest telescope in the world. William looked through the tube at very distant stars and talked to Caroline by using a speaking tube. She noted down his observations as she sat in the larger hut at the base of the telescope.

WITNESS

". . . her extraordinary powers of application in long-continued effort, with her extreme accuracy in all she did, were . . . of great practical value to my Father . . . "

"She was attached during 50 years as a second self to her brother, merging her whole existence and individuality in her desire to aid him to the entire extent and absolute devotion of her whole time and powers."
Source: John Herschel referring to his aunt, Caroline Herschel. Quoted

in *The Herschel Chronicle*, edited by Constance A. Lubbock, 1933.

"She had her reward, not only in the consciousness of being indispensable to him, but also in the universal respect and admiration which her devotion to scientific work, so unusual in a woman at that time, won her from astronomers and other men of science."
Source: Royal Society and Royal Astronomical Society, *The Scientific Papers of Sir William Herschel*, 1912.

Up, up and away

Wilbur Wright lifted the sheet of paper into the air and let it fall in front of his audience. As it floated down toward his feet, he explained why the air disturbed the paper and would not let it settle down steadily but made it flutter and dart about. He was speaking to a meeting of the Western Society of Engineers in Chicago, Illinois, in September 1901, about his interest and experiments in flight. The science of aeronautics was new and so he was not sure of the response his ideas would get. He had been working with his brother Orville and, believing that he could go no further with his work, he wrote down everything that he knew and was now passing it on to the engineers. The ideas contained in his finished writing were soon to be recognized as one of the most important contributions in the development of the study of flying.

In the last decades of the 19th century, people had developed and were flying air balloons and gliders, but no one had successfully attached a motor to a flying machine. This was the aim of the Wright brothers. Their approach to this problem, and one that made them different from others, was not only to invent an airplane but to train a pilot how to use it. The pilot had to practice controlling a glider in the air, seeing how the air affected his machine. Then, an engine could be fitted onto the machine. This would give the pilot the power to move the machine and to control it in the air.

The two brothers flew machines which they made themselves. After practicing for four years, they attached a motor to their latest machine which they called *The Flyer*. With no more audience than a few men from the local life-saving station on December 17, 1903, they tried out *The Flyer*. At the fourth attempt, the engine successfully flew the plane. They announced their achievement in a telegram they sent to their father: "Success — four flights Thursday morning all against twenty one mile wind — started from level with engine power alone — average speed through air thirty-one miles — longest 57 seconds —

Early designs for flying machines copied the wing patterns of birds, but very few ever left the ground. In 1913, the gentleman above tried to fly by attaching wings to his bicycle and making them go up and down by pedaling fast.

Many had tried to develop and fly a powered flying machine. Wilbur and Orville Wright were the first to achieve powered flight, in December 1903. From then on, they were the center of admiring crowds, as this 1908 photograph shows.

WITNESS

Airplanes could deliver goods very quickly around Britain and through Europe. This was of great advantage to the mail service. The postman, like the one in this picture taken in 1911, delivered his letters and parcels to the aerodrome where they were loaded aboard the mail plane.

inform press – home Christmas." They were the first to achieve powered flight and the news soon spread. People and their powered air machines were ready to conquer the air.

Flying became a passion for increasing numbers of people. For men, it was easier to take part in this new adventure. Many of them already had the mechanical training needed to build and maintain the early flying machines. Also, men were regarded as the ones who would take the more active role in society, leading the way and taking risks if necessary. In the past, men had always fought for their country and their family, while women looked after the home and the children. Women were at a disadvantage when it came to becoming involved in flying. They hadn't had the appropriate training, and they were expected to stand back and watch while men took part in the action, took the risks, and had the fun at the same time.

There were, however, some women who were determined and challenged society's expectations. The French Raymonde de Laroche was the first woman pilot in the world to gain a certificate in March 1910; Edith Maud in 1910 became the first British woman to fly solo in an airplane; Hilda Hewlett became the first British certified woman pilot in August 1911; and the American Harriet Quimby became the first woman to fly the English Channel in April 1912.

Now that powered flight had been achieved, it was the desire to fly longer and longer distances that spurred people on. Men and a handful of women attempted to be the first to fly to distant lands across oceans and continents. They wanted to conquer the air, and if someone had already traveled over their chosen route they would try to do it faster. The First World War showed the military value of aircraft, and their construction was improved for regular and continuous operation. With the war over and the aircraft ready, in theory it was possible to fly anywhere.

More women were by now ready to become involved in flying. They had learned new skills during the war when they were needed to work in the factories while the men were away fighting. They had also experienced a new independence, free from the constraints of looking after the home and family, and some were reluctant to give up this new freedom. They too wanted to become a part of the new world of aviation.

The record breakers

For the first time, in the 1920s, there were flights to all major parts of the world: across Africa, across Europe and India to Australia, non-stop across the United States, across the North and South Poles, and, in 1924, around the world in 15 days. One of the greatest challenges was to cross the North Atlantic Ocean. In 1919, John Alcock and Arthur Brown crossed the Atlantic in 16 hours and 27 minutes and won the $20,000 prize for the record flight from the *Daily Mail* newspaper. They were knighted by King George V. Another large amount of prize money was won by Charles Lindbergh, who in 1927 arrived in Paris from New York, after 33½ hours in a cramped cockpit. His was the first non-stop solo flight on this route. Pilots like Lindbergh became famous overnight and were guaranteed financial backing for other exploits, although getting the money to make the first flight was not always easy.

Lindbergh's flight had been paid for by a house-to-house collection in his home town, St. Louis, and so he had called his plane *Spirit of St. Louis*. When Amy Johnson, one of the British women aviators, wanted a plane to fly solo to Australia, she wondered if she could use a similar scheme and call her plane *Spirit of England*. Eventually, she was lucky enough to get sponsorship. Only the wealthy could buy their own planes. Two who had the means were Lady Heath and Lady Bailey who were among the first women to take to the air and to make milestones in women's flying. Lady Heath was the first woman to fly from the Cape of South Africa to England, which she completed between February and May 1928, and Lady Bailey was the first to fly from England to the Cape and back to England,

returning in January 1929. By the close of the 1920s, flights over all areas of the world had been achieved. All, except those by Raymonde de Laroche, Harriet Quimby, Lady Heath and Lady Bailey had been undertaken by men.

As more people became involved in flying, the newspapers became less interested in just reporting flying stories. It was not so unusual to see an airplane now or even to know someone who had flown. But as there were still fewer women involved in flying than men, women's exploits were newsworthy. In the 1920s and 1930s, it was still unusual for women to leave home and become aviators. Traditionally, it was the men who tried out new experiences first. Yet, there were women who broke the mold, and had the enthusiasm and the courage to create their own records.

Three women flyers in particular excited the public imagination in the 1930s. They were Amelia Earhart, Amy Johnson and Jean Batten. Between them, they made and broke many flying records and gave inspiration to other women and men who wanted to become involved in the fast-growing aviation business. The American Amelia Earhart had found fame when she was persuaded to be the first woman to cross the Atlantic in 1928, although it was not as the pilot but as a passenger. She proved she was a serious pilot by

Some of the pilots were treated like film and rock stars are today. Below, Charles Lindbergh arrives in Paris from New York in 1927. His plane, *Spirit of St. Louis*, had to be protected from the crowd. After her flight to Australia, Amy Johnson was also constantly surrounded by the public wherever she went.

Lady Heath was one of the first women aviators in Britain. She campaigned for women's rights to become pilots and set up a scholarship program in the late 1920s to help women learn to fly.

Women flyers made good news. Right, Amelia Earhart draws a route map for Paramount News which shows the path of her record-breaking solo flight across the Atlantic Ocean in 1932.

crossing the Atlantic solo four years later. Amy Johnson was the first woman to fly solo to Australia in 1930. She had originally taken up flying as a pastime but became an experienced flyer and then completed many record-breaking flights. Amy Johnson's Australia time record was broken by another woman, Jean Batten, who went on to hold the record for both the outward and return journeys to Australia.

These were outstanding women; they overcame the social pressures which suggested they should stay at home, and they trained to look after their airplanes as well as to fly them. They spent hour after hour flying and taking off and landing, so they would be ready to take on long flying trips. Amy Johnson had support from her parents. They accepted she was not going to get married in her early twenties and have a family. They encouraged her interest in flying and helped her with expenses. Other women could not afford the hours of training or had not gotten the educational background for the examinations. They had to be satisfied with the excitement of a trip in a plane at a fairground or watching the planes from the ground.

Air transportation

While the pioneers were breaking records, the aviation business was developing. Aircraft were being used to deliver mail and passengers. Civil flying was allowed in Britain from May 1919, and airline companies were soon formed to transport goods and passengers between certain cities. The first planes that were available to do this work were the bombers from the First World War. They were stripped of their wartime equipment and seats were installed to carry passengers.

However, these planes which would adequately carry luggage and parcels were not comfortable for the passengers. New planes were designed with more comfortable seats and more attractive interiors. But flying was still noisy and cold and passengers were often lent flying clothes to keep warm. As they were to be used on a regular basis, the planes were designed to be safer and more reliable. Uniformed crews were introduced to look after the passengers.

Today, millions of passengers a year fly in and out of Great Britain; in 1930, it was only 30,000. If women wanted to work for an airline they would usually be employed as air stewardesses, a role that even today remains very largely female. Looking after the welfare of the passengers was not unlike other roles that women were expected to perform in society, and many stewardesses were nurses. Stewardesses also undertook secretarial work, another helping role regarded as

suitable for women. The world's first stewardesses were eight women who were trained nurses, hired by an American company in 1930. They had to meet specific requirements: to be under 25 years of age, of medium build and no more than 5ft 4in (1.64m) tall.

Women found it almost impossible to get a permanent job as a pilot with either the commercial airlines or with the Air Force and their associated services. Pilots required an engineer's license and although some women did have them, they were still not taken on as pilots. In America, Amelia Earhart helped to operate one of the first regular passenger services between New York and Washington. She spoke out for women's role in aviation. She also organized and took part in the Women's Air Derby of America in 1929, which she described as "the event that started concerted activity among women fliers." After this first cross-country competition for women, the competitors (called "Petticoat Pilots," "Ladybirds" and "Flying Flappers" by the press) formed an association called the "Ninety-Nines" because of the number of founder members. They were dedicated to the improvement of women's opportunities in aviation.

Lady Heath had campaigned in Europe for the professional recognition of women pilots and had helped to bring about the cancellation of the international postwar ban on women as professional pilots. But when

Left, commercial airlines preferred to employ women as air stewardesses, to look after the passengers, rather than to pilot the planes. This is the first air stewardess, employed by Swissair in Europe, in 1934.

 **WITNESS**

"I am going to fly on one of the largest American Airlines as a co-pilot, in order to get experience . . . it will give them a good advertisement, but it's never been allowed before and you know how hard it is in this world to do something new."

"It is hard to persuade some hardboiled businessman that you have any brains behind a windowfront name. It is harder still to escape being captioned 'stunt pilot' and considered as good for nothing except to take rather unnecessary stupid risks that no ordinary mortal would dream of taking."
Source: Amy Johnson, quoted by Constance Babington Smith, *Amy Johnson*, 1967.

"There is no reason why the airplane should not open up a fruitful occupation for women. I see no reason why they cannot realize handsome incomes by carrying passengers . . . from parcel delivery, from taking photographs from above, or from conducting schools for flying."
Source: Harriet Quimby, writing c.1911. Quoted by Valerie Moolman, *Women Aloft*, 1981.

British Women! — the Royal Air Force needs your help

as CLERKS,
WAITRESSES,
COOKS, experienced
MOTOR CYCLISTS
& in many other capacities.
Full particulars from the nearest
EMPLOYMENT EXCHANGE
ENROL AT ONCE IN THE

W·R·A·F·
WOMEN'S ROYAL AIR FORCE

Above, women were encouraged to help the First World War effort by joining the Women's Royal Air Force (WRAF) in supportive roles. No mention is made of women being pilots.

Below, Air Transport Auxiliary (ATA) women pilots, 1940. Under the leadership of Pauline Gower (on left), they ferried Air Force personnel around Britain.

Amy Johnson, with all her experience, first tried to get a permanent job as a pilot in England in 1935, she was unable to find anyone to hire her. Her only promising opening in this line had come when she was given the opportunity to be a co-pilot on a scheduled flight in America two years earlier. But, this was not a permanent situation. Among the jobs that Amy Johnson had been offered in England were to take part in an Air Circus, to go on the music hall stage to lecture or to write about aviation, and to do air taxi work and joyriding.

In June 1939, she was taken on as a pilot operating the Solent air ferry. She ferried passengers, many from the army, by day and by night whenever the weather permitted. She worked at this job for nearly nine months until wartime reorganization brought it to an end. The *Daily Mirror* newspaper made much of the fact that "the world famous air pilot" was ferrying passengers at a few cents a trip. Amy Johnson felt that her fame had always made it more difficult to be taken seriously as a pilot rather than as a celebrity. The fact that she was a woman had in the past brought her great popularity but this seemed to be a disadvantage now as well. Women were still not thought to be serious pilots.

In the Second World War, a women's section of the Air Transport Auxiliary (ATA), who ferried around air force personnel, was formed. Amy Johnson at first said it was "a team of women sort of being given the crumbs to keep them quiet," but she wanted a flying job so badly that she joined them. She felt frustrated flying with the ATA, and the prejudice against women pilots was clear. The women got $900 a year compared to the men's $1,400. Amy Johnson also found that most of the men were "amateurs as against most of our women being professionals . . . we ought to have the same when we're doing precisely the same job, the same hours and the same aircraft, don't you agree? . . . It's a question of principle."

Flying career

While interviewing an Indian pilot at the London Aeroplane Club in January 1930, a reporter heard about the "lady engineer" who was working there. On the spur of the moment, he decided to interview her. Amy Johnson told the newspaper reporter that she hoped to use her recently won flying certificates to follow a career in aviation. Her first major flight was to be to Australia and she was to go alone. The reporter realized he was on to a good story.

"Girl to fly alone to Australia, the first woman air engineer and her plans" was printed in the *Evening News* and Amy Johnson's face was soon in all the London papers. She was annoyed that the reporter said she was 22 when she was really 26, that she came from the Midlands when she didn't, and that she made a comfortable living from aviation, which was not true at all. But, she used the publicity to her advantage to raise financial backing for her trip.

She had only become interested in flying when one Saturday afternoon in April 1928, she had taken a bus ride to see the airplanes at Stag Lane Aerodrome. It cost about $6.50 to join the club and the tuition was

Left, the plane for the Australia flight which was paid for by Lord Wakefield's oil company and Amy Johnson's father. Amy Johnson piloted *Jason* and carried out necessary repairs.

Above, in 1930 Amy Johnson became the first woman to fly solo from England to Australia. She was frustrated by the fact that a woman could rarely get a serious job as a pilot.

❝ WITNESS

"I want to fly to Australia, one reason being that I am certain a successful flight of this nature, by an English girl, solo and in a light plane, would do much to engender confidence amongst the public in air travel."
Source: letter from Amy Johnson to the Director of Civil Aviation, Sir Sefton Brancker, March 11, 1930, asking for support for her flight to Australia. Quoted by

Constance Babington Smith, *Amy Johnson*, 1967.

"Girls are shielded and sometimes helped so much that they lose initiative and begin to believe the signs, 'Girls don't,' and 'Girls can't,' which mark their paths."
Source: Amelia Earhart, said on occasions when she was lecturing and writing with reference to women in flying. Quoted by Valerie Moolman, *Women Aloft*, 1981.

about $2.00 per hour, but watching the activities, she decided she would put some of her $10 weekly salary aside to take flying lessons. She had only been in an airplane once, on a pleasure flight with her sister Molly near their home in Hull in 1926. They had each paid to be flown around a circuit which Amy later remarked was over too quickly. Once she started to learn to fly a plane herself, her enthusiasm grew and grew. She spent as much time as she could at the aerodrome, gaining her first pilot license by the middle of 1929 and her first engineer's license by December of the same year. She was the first woman to receive an engineer's license from the British Air Ministry and she was justly proud of it. Determined to prove her capabilities, she chose to fly solo to Australia.

Women had already flown solo to Africa. Only a navigator of long experience could successfully tackle an Atlantic flight and so the only spectacular solo flight left open to Amy Johnson was to Australia. Attempts by men to break Bert Hinkler's 15-day record which had stood since 1928 were numerous and often went unnoticed. But so far, no woman had tried to rival it.

Early in the morning on Sunday May 5, 1930, friends and relatives gathered to watch Amy Johnson and her Gipsy Moth plane called *Jason* take off for Australia. She badly underestimated the dangers in front of her. She had achieved 85 hours of flying by March 1930 but only in short bursts, an hour or two at a time. Once she was in flight and on her way to Australia, she started to experience the problems of long flights. She

In the 1920s and 1930s, conditions at landing sites were very different from today. Many could not even be called airports. Like this one, they were often clearings, perhaps in the desert or the jungle, with few or no facilities.

felt sick from the constant gasoline fumes in the cockpit. When she stopped after many hours of flying, she had to work on *Jason*'s engine and make repairs to the body. She slept only three hours a night. The aerodromes abroad were parade grounds, running tracks, fields and runways cut into the jungle, with little or no equipment and no one who spoke English. She was also unprepared for the vast mountains, the sandstorms, and the burning heat of the desert.

When she arrived in India after six days of flying, she realized she had broken Hinkler's previous record by two days. She was delighted. But as problems set in during the later stages of her journey, she knew she couldn't break his Australia record. She wrote to her parents, "I am getting very tired of my trip and a wee bit discouraged because everything seems to be going wrong . . . yet I am absolutely convinced that I have been watched over the whole way. I have had several narrow escapes and I am gratefully thankful for my safety even though my plans have all been spoilt. (sic)"

Although she was disappointed, her spirits revived when she realized people recognized her achievement. People around the world had been watching her progress and many came to greet her when she touched down in Port Darwin, Australia.

In the public eye

When Amy Johnson arrived in Australia on May 24, 1930, she was very tired and disappointed. She had not broken the record flight to Australia but the world didn't seem to care. Enormous crowds came to meet her and messages of congratulations on her solo flight poured in from around the world. They came from relatives, friends, strangers, celebrities, politicians and royalty. Everybody wanted to meet her. She attended receptions, balls, galas, rallies, posed, gave interviews, and received many gifts. Her new life as a public figure was a surprise to her but it thrilled her. She reacted to the public attention with great patience and natural charm, and this made the crowds love her even more.

Amy Johnson had risen suddenly from obscurity to fame. Her success seemed to put flying within everyone's reach. As details began to emerge of her background, the fact that she was from an ordinary family in Hull, that she had worked hard to pay for her lessons and spent every moment she could at the aerodrome, made people think she was not very different from them. Amy Johnson was different from the titled ladies who were usually in the news for their flying. She was not rich like they were. She had succeeded by hard work and determination.

In fact, Amy Johnson was quite an unusual woman in her strength of character, her ability to carry out her plans and the fact that she had been to a university and was now a trained engineer. But when the public applauded her achievements, she reacted with such friendliness that they all felt they knew her. Songs and verses were written to honor her. They were the hits of the day. The titles included "Amy," "Aeroplane Girl," "Queen of the Air," and "Johnnie, Heroine of the Air."

Amy Johnson received more attention than another person flying the same course may have gotten. It was not a particularly pioneering flight. It was the ninth of its kind. Nor did her flight prove that it could be done solo; Bert Hinkler had done that already. It was the fact that the flight had been achieved by a woman that was important. She was the thirty-seventh woman to receive an aviator's certificate in Britain, but before she made her Australia flight there had been very few

Everyone wanted to meet Amy Johnson once she arrived in Australia. She was given many presents, including this MG sports car, complete with a model of her plane. She was so popular and her appointment book was so full that she didn't return to England for two months.

" WITNESS

"I cannot realize it yet. I feel a person apart from all this — I seem to be looking on at someone else whom the world is acclaiming."
Source: Amy Johnson, on how it felt to be a world-famous figure overnight, 1930. Quoted by Constance Babington Smith, *Amy Johnson*, 1967.

"I admit that I am a woman, and the first one to do it . . . but in the future I do
not want it to be unusual that women should do things; I want it to be recognized that women can do them."
Source: Amy Johnson in a radio broadcast soon after her return to England in August 1930, after her Australia flight. Quoted in same book as above.

When Amy Johnson arrived in Australia after her record-breaking flight, she instantly became a celebrity. The Wakefield Oil Company had paid many of her costs. They were eager to advertise her success, which would also sell their oil.

achievements of this type in the history of women's flying. One of the outstanding women pilots, Lady Heath, who made the first flight by a woman from the Cape of South Africa to England, was asked to comment on Amy Johnson's Australian flight. She said, "Miss Johnson's flight was easily the finest ever performed by a woman."

Amy Johnson enjoyed all the attention that her Australia flight brought her. Everyone was so keen to meet her that she stayed in Australia for two months touring around the country. When she did return to England, the public had not forgotten her. She was congratulated on behalf of the women of Britain and handed her fan mail. A 12-mile procession took her at snail's pace into the center of London. The next morning, the public was still keen to meet her. This was to go on for the rest of her life. She loved the public attention but cherished even more the honors she received from her colleagues, who had a better understanding of her skills as a pilot and engineer.

From 1934 to 1937, she was the President of the Women's Engineering Society. During this time, she was also awarded the gold medal of the Royal Aero Club. But she never seemed happier than when she was acting as a pilot for the Air Transport Auxiliary, ferrying planes and dispatches around England when the Second World War broke out. She was being paid as a pilot and had no special treatment as a celebrity, although she still enjoyed it when she landed at a Royal Air Force airfield and the airmen would recognize her, immediately surround her and ask for her autograph. But this part of her life was not to last very long. She knew the type of work she did was dangerous; she was flying all hours of the day and night and trying to avoid enemy aircraft. She predicted that her love of flying would kill her, as it had many other women flyers, including Raymonde de Laroche, Harriet Quimby and Amelia Earhart, and it did. While ferrying a plane for the Air Ministry in early 1941, she and her plane disappeared over the Thames estuary.

BIOGRAPHY

1903 Born July 1 at Kingston-upon-Hull, to herring importers.
1925 Graduates from the University of Sheffield with a B.A. in Economics, Latin and French.
1925 Moves to London to take up a secretarial job.
1928 Spends all her spare time at Stag Lane, Edgware, the home of the London Aeroplane Club.
1929 Granted her pilot's license and later her ground engineer's license.
1930 May 5, leaves Croydon for Australia in *Jason*. May 10, arrives at Karachi. May 24, arrives at Port Darwin, Australia. June 3, appointed Commander of the British Empire.
Awarded the Egyptian gold medal for valor, and the women's trophy of the International League of Aviators.
1931 July, flies across Siberia to Tokyo in record-breaking time. The return journey is also a record.
Receives the President's gold medal of the Society of Engineers.
1932 Marries Jim Mollison, also a record-breaking pilot. Breaks her husband's record for a solo flight to Cape Town. The return journey is also a record.
1933 Flies non-stop with her husband from England to Connecticut.
1934 Husband and wife make a record flight to Karachi.
1934–1937 Becomes President of the Women's Engineering Society.
1936 May, solo flight to the Cape when she beats the records for both flights and for the double journey. Awarded the gold medal of the Royal Aero Club. Marriage dissolved.
1939 Joins the Air Transport Auxiliary.
1941 January 5, lost over the Thames estuary when ferrying a plane for the Air Ministry. No body found.
1943 December, death presumed.

LAST FRONTIER

Lunar landing

". . . I'm at the foot of the ladder. The LM [lunar module] footpads are only depressed in the surface about one or two inches . . . It's almost like a powder . . . I'm going to step off the LM now . . . That's one small step for man, one giant leap for mankind." With these words, Neil Armstrong stepped out of the dish-shaped landing pad and onto the surface of the Moon. He was the first human being to walk on any surface other than Earth's. Around the world, millions of people were watching him step into history. At the control center in Houston, it was just before 10 pm on a Sunday evening in July 1969. The pictures of Neil Armstrong on the Moon were broadcast live to homes and movie screens all around the world.

Nineteen minutes later, it was Edwin "Buzz" Aldrin's turn to step onto the lunar surface. They both found it easy to move around; their boots sank only a little into the lunar dust. The effect of the Moon's gravity, only one sixth of the Earth's, was much less inhibiting than they had expected. The task for these astronauts was to go to the Moon, land, come back and report on the nature of the environment. The two men spent over two hours on the lunar surface and brought back to Earth about 45 lbs (22 kg) of lunar rock samples.

With the subsequent American moon missions in the 1970s, the list of American astronauts who had been in orbit or landed on the Moon grew and grew. The list didn't, however, include any women astronauts. There was no reason to believe that women were inspired by the space program any less than men. They had explored and uncovered the secrets of their own planet as well as men. Women had traveled by land, sea and air to all parts of the Earth. They had been on expeditions to remote parts of Africa and South America, crossing hot deserts and steaming jungle, and had

After the first human being landed on the Moon in 1969, many more successful trips to the Moon were made by American astronauts in the 1970s. But women could not even apply to be astronauts. The exploration of the unknown and the adventure were reserved for men.

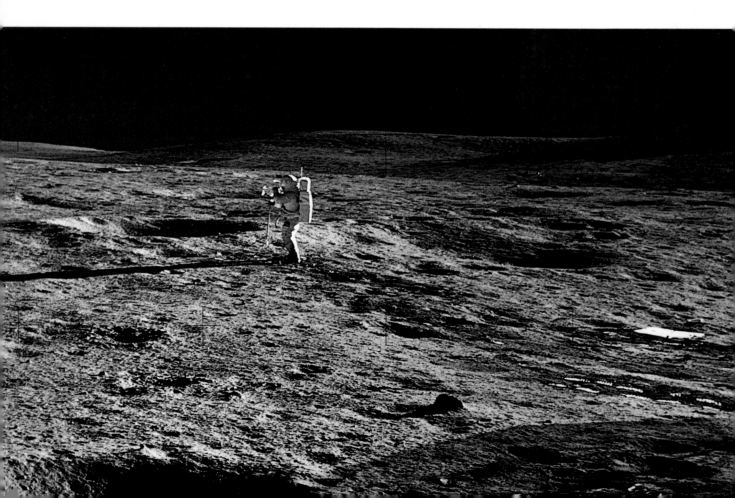

journeyed across the cold icy wastelands of the north and south polar regions. However, none seemed to be involved in exploring space. The American men and women paid for their space missions with their taxes, but women were not actively involved in conquering space.

The 1940s and 1950s saw increasing numbers of women going out to work. As they asserted their independence and showed how capable they were at their jobs, they looked forward to having a greater choice in the work available to them. Some women weren't satisfied with low-grade jobs, or the work that was traditionally left to the women, such as nursing and secretarial. They wanted to be air pilots, doctors and managers. At the same time, female students were encouraged by their teachers to show that they could succeed in their subjects as well as male students. Women were driving cars, becoming involved in local community life, and making their voices heard on national issues.

Gradually, women began to be offered the same opportunities as men, but in some areas it was not automatic and women had to push hard to be heard, and to be treated equally with men. In the 1960s and 1970s, they demanded equal rights from their employers and from politicians, and, when it was necessary to further their course, they demonstrated in the streets.

There was a small group of women who wanted the chance to travel into space. They were grouped around Jerrie Cobb, an aircraft executive, who had been flying planes since the age of 12 and who had won many awards and set records. The 13 women were all experienced pilots. When Jerrie Cobb heard that the Soviet Union had a program for training women for space flight, she went to Washington to plead with the politicians for a similar program.

Another woman in the group, Jane Briggs Hart, was married to a politician and flew him around on his business. She managed to see the Vice President of the United States to try to persuade him to let women join the astronaut team. Congressional hearings were set up to investigate the role of women in space but none of this had any immediate effect. These women pilots never had the chance to become astronauts and were later known as the "Forgotten 13." It wasn't until the 1980s that the first American woman, Sally Ride, traveled into space.

When the *Apollo II* astronaut crew, including Neil Armstrong and Buzz Aldrin who were the first human beings to walk on the Moon, returned to Earth they were greeted as heroes. Here, they are sitting on the trunk of the front car, being greeted by the New York crowds.

 **WITNESS**

The President of the United States talking from the White House to Armstrong and Aldrin on the Moon:
". . . this certainly has to be the most historic telephone call ever made. I just can't tell you how proud we all are . . . And for people all over the world, I am sure that they too join with Americans in recognizing what an immense feat this is. Because of what you have done, the heavens have become a part of man's world."
Source: Gene Farmer, Dora Jane Hamblin, *First on the Moon, A Voyage with Neil Armstrong, Michael Collins, Edwin E. Aldrin Jr.,* 1970.

"Women will travel in space just as surely as men. It's only a question of when. Women have engaged in all phases of aviation to date, including ballooning, gliding, parachuting and powered flight. There is no reason to believe that women will be eliminated now that we are leaving the atmosphere and getting into space."
Source: J. Cochran to J. Cobb, letter March 23, 1962. From *A Salute to Women in Aerospace,* unpublished compilation by Lillian D. Kozloski, National Air and Space Museum, Washington.

The space age

The President of the United States, John F. Kennedy, said in May 1961, "I believe that this nation should commit itself to achieving the goal, before the decade is out, of landing a man on the Moon and returning him safely to Earth." He said this only 20 days after Alan Shepard, America's first astronaut, had been launched into space and less than four years after the world's first spacecraft, the Russian *Sputnik 1*, had been launched. The goal was realized when the gap between Earth and Moon was bridged in 1969.

The idea of men and women traveling in space does not seem as strange today as it did in the 1950s. The space scientists who developed the first rockets didn't know how safe space travel would be and they were unsure what effect it would have on human beings. The risks are fewer than they used to be but even with our present more advanced technology and knowledge, things can still go wrong. In early 1986, the Space Shuttle *Challenger* exploded soon after take-off, killing all crew members on board. Rockets and equipment can be tested without harm to people, but there is only one way of finding out how space travel really affects a human, and that is to send a person into space. On November 3, 1957, the first living creature (and the first female) was sent into space; she was a black and white fox terrier, called Laika. Her survival showed that there was no serious problem facing space travelers. Other dogs and monkeys were launched and monitored by both the Russians and the Americans before a human was sent into space.

The first person was a Russian man, Yuri Gagarin, who was launched on April 12, 1961. In these early years of the space age, two countries dominated the space industry. They were the Soviet Union and the United States and there was always a race between them to see who could do what first. The first American was Alan Shepard, who flew on May 5, 1961. The early astronauts all had the same type of flying background. Gagarin was from the Russian airforce, while Shepard and the first moonwalkers, Armstrong and Aldrin, were from the American armed services.

It was impossible in the United States for a woman even to get the chance to be chosen and trained as an astronaut. When the government body carrying out America's space program, the National Aeronautics and Space Administration (NASA), was established in 1958, it decreed that all astronaut applicants had to be male. Jet pilot experience was also a requirement,

Above, the Soviet Union included women in their cosmonaut training program from the early 1960s. In 1963, the Russian Valentina Tereshkova was the first woman to travel into space.

and as at this time women were also prohibited from undergoing military jet flight training, they were totally barred from becoming astronauts. By contrast, in Russia, three women were in the cosmonaut (a Russian astronaut) training team in 1962. One of these, Valentina Tereshkova, was to be the first-ever woman in space in June 1963. Her flight lasted almost three days. This was longer than the total time spent in space by the first six American astronauts, if not as long as the flights of two of her male colleagues.

The role of the very earliest astronauts was to act as pilots if necessary, but mainly to act as "guinea-pigs," human specimens in space so that the scientists on Earth could study the effects of space travel. As our knowledge of space and its effects and uses has grown, so humankind has changed and adapted the space program. At the beginning of the space age in the late 1950s and early 1960s, there was a desire to conquer space by sending up humans. When a man landed on the Moon, the dream was realized. This was

Male or female, all astronauts and cosmonauts undergo extensive training before they are launched into space. Left, two Russian cosmonauts practice their routines.

In the 1960s and early 1970s, women could work for NASA but not as astronauts. Yet, the launch control room in the Kennedy Space Center, above, was very male-dominated.

followed by scientific investigation of other planets by launching space probe machines while the humans stayed on Earth.

At the same time, satellites were developed which could be launched into space to help people on Earth to communicate or send information, such as TV pictures, more cheaply and more quickly. For these different types of activity in space, different space vehicles and also different space specialists were needed. With the introduction of the Space Shuttle into the American space program in the mid 1970s, the door was finally opened to women astronauts.

The Space Shuttle required a crew to work alongside the astronaut pilot. This meant that the qualifications needed to be an astronaut were moving away from the high performance flight experience and concentrating more on the educational background. The women who wanted to be astronauts could now be compared to the male candidates on an equal basis.

" WITNESS

"In 1962, when several women pilots sought a congressional hearing to push for female participation as astronauts, NASA trotted out its most famous name — John Glenn — to testify. On July 17, 1962, . . . he said: 'The men go off and fight the wars and fly the airplanes and come back and help design and build and test them. The fact that women are not in this field is a fact of our social order.'"
Source: *Washington Post,* June 24, 1983.

"'I fussed and fumed and went to see Vice President Johnson . . .' She testified at the hearings that women had 'the right stuff' but John Glenn disagreed saying: 'If we can find any women that demonstrate that they have better qualifications than the men around them, we would welcome them with open arms.'"
Source: Jane Briggs Hart, quoted by R. Wheeler, P. Snowdon, "American Women in Space," *Journal of the British Interplanetary Society,* 1987.

Science in space

Space is a very costly business. The *Apollo* series of spacecraft which took men to the Moon and brought them back again cost a total of $24,000,000,000. On each occasion, most of the *Saturn* rockets which launched them, and the *Apollo* spacecraft which transported them, were discarded, and what did return to Earth never flew again. The Space Shuttle was conceived to reduce the cost of space travel. It is part rocket, part spacecraft and part aircraft. It is the first reusable spacecraft that can shuttle backward and forward from nearby space to Earth. The Shuttle is very versatile. It can take spacecraft into orbit and launch them from its payload bay (the cargo area), take a space station into orbit, retrieve satellites and return them to Earth, and act as a mini-space factory.

When the Space Shuttle flies, four types of astronaut fly in it: a commander, a pilot, mission specialists, who are concerned with the job, or mission, on a particular Shuttle flight, and payload specialists, who are responsible for the use of the experiments and instruments in the payload bay. The first three types are chosen from NASA's astronauts in training. The last type does not undergo intensive astronaut training.

In 1976, NASA issued a call for astronauts for the Shuttle and women were encouraged to apply. By this time, women were working in all kinds of jobs. There was no reason for anyone to think that they could not do the jobs in space. This changing social outlook and gradual loss of prejudice, together with the ability of the Space Shuttle to regularly carry a mixed crew of up to seven, with some privacy during missions, changed the criteria for crew selection. Out of the 659 people who wanted to be pilot astronauts, eight were women but none were chosen. A total of 5,680 applicants wanted to be mission specialists; 1,251 of these were women. When the successful candidates were announced in 1978, six of the 35 chosen were women.

The Shuttle projects depend for their success on the skills of the mission specialist scientists. They all have to be highly trained scientists who can monitor and interpret the scientific experiments on board the Shuttle. They will play a key role in NASA's next major project, the establishment of a permanent station in orbit, where men and women can work for months at a time. Their backgrounds reflect the wide range of necessary talents. Sally Ride is a trained physicist; the other five women who were chosen with her are a surgeon, a physician, a biochemist, a geologist, and an electrical engineer.

The mission specialists, male and female, all follow the same intensive training which includes hundreds of hours of practice time in a model spacecraft, and they help to develop the Shuttle's equipment. Even then, it is not certain that they will be chosen to fly in a Shuttle mission. Sally Ride was assigned to the team which was to design a remote manipulator arm, for the

Left, the American Space Shuttle can carry a scientific laboratory (Spacelab) into space. As a result, some of the astronauts need to be specialists in the instrumentation carried on board. One of these specialists, Sally Ride, is shown here working with other crew members.

Right, it is impossible to lie down in space in a conventional bed as there is no gravity. This sleep restraint is Sally Ride's bed and keeps her from floating around. Other things are specially designed to work in this space environment, too, such as food, and washing and toilet facilities.

"The President [Mr. Reagan] told Dr. Ride: 'Let me just remind you that when you were at the White House, somebody said that the best man for the job was a woman.' Referring to her use of the craft's robotic arm to retrieve scientific instruments in orbit, Mr. Reagan said '. . . you were there for one reason: because you were the best person for the job.'"
Source: telephone call from Reagan immediately after *Challenger* landing, *New York Times*, June 25, 1983.

"Because we had a new spacecraft, and it was going to be built so that it had space inside it . . . and could have toilet facilities that could accommodate women . . . and I think, because at that time in our country people were feeling a little bit bad about the way they had treated women . . . they said, 'It's a federal job and we're going to open it to all races, sexes, religious backgrounds and ages,' she said."
Source: Carolyn L. Huntoon, Johnson Space Center's deputy chief for personnel development, on NASA's call for mission specialists, *The Washington Post*, May 9, 1983.

Above, in 1984, for the first time, two astronauts retrieved two satellites to be brought back to Earth. They were helped in their operation by the remote manipulator arm (right) designed by Sally Ride. It was operated by Anna Fisher from inside the Space Shuttle.

deployment and retrieval of satellites. It was because of her expertise in this area, and her flair for solving difficult engineering problems, that she was chosen to take part in the seventh Shuttle mission in June 1983.

The other women selected in 1978 developed their own specialist skills. Rhea Seddon, the physician, dealt with Shuttle medical subjects and flight nutrition, as well as serving as a rescue helicopter physician. Kathy Sullivan, the geologist, continued her interest in the study of the Earth. When she flew with Sally Ride in October 1984 on an eight-day Shuttle mission, in order to observe the Earth, she became the first American woman to go on EVA (Extra Vehicular Activity), that is, to walk in space outside the Space Shuttle.

Women in space

When the six women were chosen in 1978 to train to be mission specialist astronauts, this marked the final abandonment of NASA's military pilot-orientated selection requirements. It had taken almost 20 years for NASA to accept that women as well as men could be astronauts. America could have had the first woman in space as early as 1960, when the woman pilot Jerrie Cobb successfully underwent the same physical examinations as the seven male astronauts training at the time. The medical examination proved she was physically and mentally capable of withstanding the rigors of space flight.

Twelve more American women, all experienced pilots with impressive qualifications, underwent and passed the tests by 1961. They had the tests carried out privately, but by the doctor who tested the men. Most of the costs were covered by another female pilot, Jacqueline Cochran. In 1953, she had become the first woman in the world to exceed the speed of sound. By now, her active days were over but she supported women's attempts to travel into space. She advocated

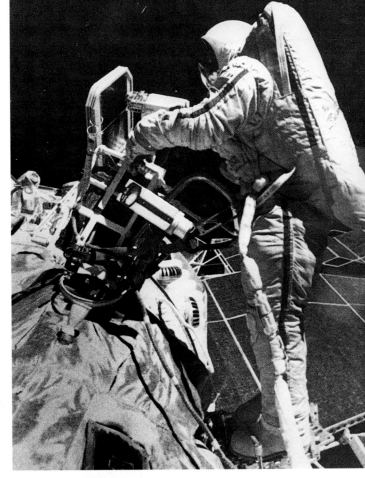

Above, astronauts are occasionally required to walk outside their spaceship, in the space environment. The space "walk" is called Extra Vehicular Activity (EVA). The first woman to do this was the Russian Svetlana Savitskaya, in 1984.

Left, Jerrie Cobb, an experienced pilot and an aircraft executive who campaigned for American women to be accepted for astronaut training in the 1960s. Cobb showed that there was no physical reason why women should not be chosen when, in 1960, she passed the same physical examinations taken by the male astronauts.

taking things slowly, believing that as the space plans developed, so women candidates would be accepted. Others were not so easily satisfied.

Attitudes toward accepting women astronauts were not changing, although women were employed in other ways by NASA. Since the 1960s, women had taken part in ground-based experiments and provided different types of support. Although Jerrie Cobb could not persuade the American government and NASA to take on female astronauts, in 1961 she was appointed to advise NASA officials on any programs including women. She later commented that "she was the most unconsulted consultant of any government body." The support that women still provide today covers technical, administrative, scientific and engineering areas. The statistics show that 25% of NASA's total staff are female, but they account for only around 6% of the scientists and engineers. NASA points out that this figure is above the national average.

There have never been any physical or mental reasons for excluding women from the astronaut program. The "Forgotten 13" had proved this. The different physical make-up of a woman causes no problem to her or to the accommodation arrangements in the Shuttle cabin. Even the spacesuits are no longer tailor-made to fit one person. By the time Sally Ride flew in 1983, she, like the men, used a suit off the rack, developed for human use, male or female. The only changes made in the spacecraft to accommodate her were an increase in the adjustability of the seats because of her shorter limbs, the addition of a curtain across the vacuum toilet chamber (although Sally Ride didn't ask for this), and changes in the grooming aids supplied to the astronauts. She did not need the shaving kit.

Sally Ride's flight in space firmly established an equal role for women in the space exploration program. They have the same opportunities as the men to apply for astronaut jobs, they undergo the same training, and, like the men, are chosen to fly if they can do the job. Women now make up 10% of the astronaut corps. This figure reflects the number of female applicants, rather than a bias. If more women apply to be astronauts, more are likely to be chosen. As far as NASA is concerned, the assignment of women to Shuttle crews today is a routine matter based on ability and need, and is no longer a cause for notice.

Yet Sally Ride and the other women astronauts accept that they are role models for other women and girls, and that for some time to come they will be watched by the public more closely than their male colleagues.

In 1978, NASA chose women for the first time to train to be astronauts. There were six of them. Several more have been chosen since then. The first black woman to be chosen was Dr. Mae Jemison. She was one of 15 new candidates presented to the press in August 1987, before starting the training program.

WITNESS

"'Now that Sally Ride is flying and the rest of us will be flying later on, I think NASA has proved it is serious about putting women into space; that we weren't simply taken in for training and not considered serious competitors,' said physician astronaut Rhea Seddon."

"'It's a symbol that society is opening up and that there are many more options available to women,' said engineer astronaut Mary Cleave, 36, who learned to fly before she could drive the family car."
Source: *The Washington Times,* June 14, 1983.

SALLY RIDE

First woman

When Sally Ride opened the newspaper, she saw an announcement that NASA was accepting astronaut applications. She looked at the long list of qualifications and thought, "I'm one of those people." Little more than six years later, in 1983, she became the first American woman to fly in space. Newspaper and television people desperately searched for any details about this first woman. She was the first astronaut since Neil Armstrong walked on the Moon to be so besieged by the media. There were hundreds of requests for interviews from around the world. Twice the usual number of women journalists who turn out for a Shuttle launch journeyed to the Kennedy Space Center in Florida to cover this event. Nothing, it seemed, symbolized the progress of American women in the past decade quite so well as the sight of a female astronaut climbing toward the stars.

Throughout, Sally Ride maintained her composure. She gave few interviews and guarded her privacy. The fact that she was the first American woman in space was not as important to her as her role as a pioneer mission specialist. She had not joined the space program in order to be the first woman in space. She had gotten her job as a scientist, and not as a woman scientist. Just before she flew, she said, "What I intend to do is just do what I've been trained to do — do as good a job as I can when I'm up there and hope that provides a good role model." Yet she readily admitted that she was a beneficiary of the women's movement, although she wasn't an active participant in it. "My selection as an astronaut would not have happened without the women's movement."

She had been chosen for this crew by its commander Robert Crippen because she was "the very best person for the job." Before joining NASA, Sally Ride had trained as a physicist at Stanford University. This background gave her the educational requirements for her job as a mission specialist. When she joined NASA, she started to specialize in a part of the Shuttle program.

She spent three years developing and acquiring complete knowledge of the Shuttle's 15m mechanical arm (Remote Manipulator System) which she and fellow crew member John Fabian were to test. Together, during the flight, they used this to test the Shuttle's ability to retrieve and return satellites to orbit, once they had done onboard repairs. The arm hoisted a specially designed payload out of the cargo bay, tossed it overboard, and Ride and Fabian used the arm

Sally Ride was the first American woman to fly in space, in June 1983 aboard the *Challenger* Space Shuttle. She received much attention as the first woman but she felt that what was more important was to do a good job.

to bring it back on board. The test was an unqualified success. Her other designated tasks were to deploy two communications satellites, perform or monitor about 40 scientific experiments and repair malfunctioning equipment, as well as assist the commander and the pilot during ascent, re-entry and landing.

During Sally Ride's time at NASA, from 1978 to 1987, only a few days were spent in flight; she also acted as a communicator, passing instructions between the

Left, on the *Challenger* Space Shuttle flight in June 1983, Sally Ride worked as a mission specialist and tested the Shuttle's mechanical arm (Remote Manipulator System). Here she is communicating with ground control on Earth.

Below, the Space Shuttle *Challenger* carried Sally Ride into space twice, in June 1983 and October 1984. The crew's cabin is at the front of the vehicle. The payload bay that carries the cargo of satellites, laboratory equipment or instrumentation is in the middle.

Johnson Space Center and astronauts in flight; as the only astronaut in the team that investigated the *Challenger* Shuttle disaster; and she developed NASA space programs for the future.

Her ideas about the future role of Americans in space were presented to NASA, and in February 1988, the President of the United States endorsed its contents. The report has become known as the Ride report after its main author. The way ahead for the Americans includes returning astronauts to the Moon and then, by the early years of the 21st century, landing them on Mars. Sally Ride, however, has decided to leave her astronaut job at NASA and return to research work at Stanford University. Even though she is an accomplished scientist, most people know Sally Ride as a successful woman astronaut. She has said, "It's too bad that society isn't to the point yet where the country could just send up a woman astronaut and nobody would think twice about it."

" WITNESS

"Although Dr. Ride, who joined the astronaut corps in 1978, has repeatedly insisted that she did not enter the space program 'to become a historic figure or a symbol of progress for women,' her achievements as an astronaut and astrophysicist and her unshakable self-confidence and composure have made her, virtually overnight, one of the most famous and respected women in the country and a role model for thousands of girls the world over."
Source: *Current Biography* journal, 1983.

"'I'm very honored NASA chose me to be the first woman,' she said, laughing agreeably at the question, then stressing she was more excited to be getting her chance to fly, than she was to be the first woman to do so."
Source: Sally Ride, *Los Angeles Times*, May 13, 1982.

In the public eye

Commander Robert Crippen, pilot Frederik Hauck, and mission specialists John Fabian and Sally Ride, four of the five crew members that would take part on the seventh Shuttle flight, were gathered to face the press. Crippen introduced his crew and Ride laughed good-naturedly at his description of her as "undoubtedly the prettiest member of the flight crew." This was the crew's first joint public news conference; others were to follow which included the final crew member Norman Thagard, the physician and third mission specialist. As the first woman in space, and the only woman member of this *Challenger* crew, Sally Ride received much more than her fair share of the questions.

She deftly fielded questions about her emotional stability and her suitability for the mission. When asked if she would wear a bra in outer space, she replied, "There is no sag in Zero G (gravity)." She was asked if she wept when she had a problem. "Why doesn't someone ask Rick (Hauck) those questions?" she responded. Someone asked if she thought she would be watched more closely than other astronauts because she was a woman. Sally Ride passed the question back, saying, "It seems to me I ought to be asking you that question."

At the press conferences, which were held before and after Sally Ride's flight, the first American woman in space was asked questions that were more to do with her being a woman than an astronaut. The text tells how she responded and the "Witness" shows how the Commander of the crew replied to such questions.

The astronauts were also asked about the fact that she is female: would she be an inconvenience? Crippen replied, "Sally's been anything but an inconvenience." And when Hauck was asked if he minded the fact that Sally Ride was getting all the media attention, he said, "I didn't join this program to get media attention, but now that I'm flying with Sally I'm getting too much."

Sally Ride and the crew came to realize that she would be accepted as a role model, even though it is not what she intended to be. About her breaking of the gender barrier, she says, "I honestly don't have time to think about it." It was obvious that once the questions moved away from make-up, privacy and her husband, and became more technical, Sally Ride the scientist was pleased.

NASA did not emphasize the "first woman" element of the *Challenger* flight too much. They included it as one of the facts that they mentioned to the press, along with a number of other firsts. This was the first five-member crew, the largest launched up till then. It was the first time the mechanical arm would be used. It was the first flight to carry a doctor on board to study space sickness. It was also to be the first time the Shuttle would land in Florida. As it happened, bad

BIOGRAPHY

1951 Born May 26, Sally Kristen Ride, in Encino, California. Father is political science professor.
1973–1978 Graduates from Stanford University with a B.Sc. in physics and a B.A. in English (1973), an M.S. in physics (1975) and a Ph.D. in physics (1978).
1977 Answers NASA ad for mission specialists.
1978 January, selected as first female astronaut.
1979 August, completes a one-year training period; is eligible for assignment as a mission specialist.
1981 November, and
1982 March, serves as a capsule communicator for Space Shuttle flights 2 and 3, relaying instructions from the flight director to the spacecraft crew.

1982 July, marries fellow astronaut and astronomer Steven A. Hawley.
1983 June 18 to June 24, first flight in space in Challenger Space Shuttle. First American woman to orbit the Earth; first person to perform release and capture of satellites with 50ft robotic arm, Remote Manipulator System (RMS).
1984 October 5, second flight on Challenger, eight-day mission to study the Earth's environment.
1986 Member of NASA's Space Leadership Planning Group and Strategic Planning Council, essentially NASA's management.
1987 Marriage dissolved.
1987 May, returns to Stanford University.

Sally Ride and the *Challenger* crew, 1983. A Space Shuttle crew has to live and work closely together while in orbit. Once back on the ground, they also work together.

weather in the end prevented the landing in Florida and *Challenger* returned to California.

After *Challenger*'s return, Sally Ride was still the focus of attention. There were ceremonies, receptions and press conferences, but she pointedly refused all invitations that did not include her fellow crew members. She did not wish to be treated any differently from her male colleagues.

However, this was not the way the press and public saw it. The press continued to write articles about her being the first American woman in space. She was hailed as a modern day heroine on the television. NASA officials were also besieged by business people requesting licenses to sell posters and other goods bearing Sally Ride's name and image. The requests were turned down. At the Shuttle lift-off, however, many of the several hundred thousand spectators wore T-shirts with the message "Ride, Sally Ride."

WITNESS

"The requirements for astronauts in the space program have changed perhaps more than the social order has. Consider the kind of questions Ride had to put up with from the press: Would the flight affect her reproductive organs? Did she intend to become a mother after her flight? Does she weep when things go wrong in flight simulations?"
Source: *Washington Post*, June 24, 1983.

"At one point a visibly annoyed Commander Crippen told one journalist, as reported in Maclean's *magazine (June 27, 1983), 'She is flying with us because she is the very best person for the job. There is no man I would rather have in her place.'"*
Source: from the crew's first joint public news conference, mid-May 1982, quoted in *Current Biography* journal, 1983.

Conclusion

The three women discussed in this book have all worked in areas that involved exploring the unknown. The three areas have been quite different but each of them found that the fact that they were women caused them difficulty and brought more attention to their achievements.

Caroline Herschel worked in astronomy, discovering previously unknown comets and cataloging the stars to make the heavens more familiar for astronomers to come. Her work was greatly appreciated by her male colleagues but she was not fully accepted in their circle. However, this was not something that upset Caroline Herschel. These were the social attitudes of the time, which she accepted. She did not expect anything, and so she was not disappointed.

Amy Johnson, however, did not like the double standards in aviation in the 1930s. She was one of the "record breaking" pilots that traveled previously unknown routes across the world. As she was one of the few women doing this, the public was always interested in her exploits. Yet she found, away from the limelight, that it was difficult to be accepted as a serious pilot. Her male colleagues were readily accepted as regular pilots with a good wage, but even where women were accepted, their pay was lower than the men's.

Between the time of Amy Johnson and Sally Ride, the equality between the sexes improved enormously in many areas. This was largely due to women in all walks of life asking for fair chances and opportunities. The astronaut Sally Ride was chosen for her work in the unknown because she was the best person for the job. She continues to work as a physicist in a field in which it is a person's qualifications, and not sex, that count. But would-be women astronauts had to wait a long time for these equal opportunities.

Although these three women came from very different backgrounds and from different times, they were all pioneers of the unknown. In their different ways, they achieved success in their chosen professions by overcoming prejudice against women in those fields. They all achieved because of hard work, determination and courage. They showed the way into the unknown for others, and continue to be role models who inspire other women to follow their lead.

BOOKS TO READ

Amelia Earhart by Blythe Randolph, Franklin Watts, 1987

Exploring with a Telescope by Glenn F. Chaple, Jr. Franklin Watts, 1988

Flying Safe? by Christopher Lampton, Franklin Watts, 1983

Great American Astronauts by Karen O'Connor, Franklin Watts, 1988

Space Explorers by Gregory Vogt, Franklin Watts, 1988

Space Ships by Gregory Vogt, Franklin Watts, 1988

The Story of the Space Shuttle by Tim Furniss, David & Charles, 1986

To Space and Back by Susan Oakie and Sally Ride Lothrop, William Morrow, 1986

Going into the unknown takes great courage and determination. Caroline Herschel, Amy Johnson and Sally Ride all worked in the realms of the unknown. Today, there are women working in astronomy and aviation, and in these areas they have helped to answer many questions. But there is still a lot to learn about space.

Time chart

1781 England
The planet Uranus is discovered. This radically changes people's view of our surroundings in space, and brings fame for the discoverer William Herschel and his sister assistant **Caroline Herschel**.

1820 England
The Royal Astronomical Society is founded. **Caroline Herschel** and **Mary Somerville** are accepted members of the scientific community. **Margaret Bryan** and **Janet Taylor** publish astronomical works.

1890–1920 Europe
Women start to receive a more systematic education as girls' schools and colleges are founded. They also become university students in the 1860s in Switzerland, 1870s in England, 1880s in France and 1900s in Germany.

1900s United States
Wilbur and Orville Wright achieve powered flight in 1903. In 1906, **Lillian Todd** is the first American woman to design and build an airplane. In 1911, **Harriet Quimby** and **Matilde Moisant** are the first to get their pilot's license.

1910–1930 England
Women push for equality. **Emmeline Pankhurst** campaigns for equal votes for women. **Hilda Hewlett**, the first English woman to gain her pilot's license, instructs First World War fighter pilots.

1939–1945 Europe
In the war, the Russians **Marina Raskova** and **Valentina Grizodubova** lead regiments of flyers and bombers, the German pilots **Melitta Schiller** and **Hanna Reitsch** test advanced fighters, and 100 English women fly for the ATA.

1945 England
Marjory Stephenson and **Kathleen Lonsdale** are the first women scientists to be full members of the Royal Society. **Lise Meitner** is elected to the Berlin Academy (1949), and **Yvonne Choquet-Bruhat** to the Paris Academy (1979).

1960s Russia
After Yuri Gagarin's first space flight in 1961, **Valentina Tereshkova** undergoes training and becomes the first woman in space on June 16, 1963, in the spaceship Vostok VI.

1960–1970 United States
American women campaign hard, but unsuccessfully, to be astronauts in the space program. The "Forgotten 13" include **Jerrie Cobb** and the experienced pilot twins **Jan** and **Marion Dietrich**.

1983 United States
The first American woman astronaut, **Sally Ride**, flies into space. Other women follow her, including **Anna Fisher**, the first mother in space, and **Shannon Lucid**, who at first tried to become a commercial pilot.

1980s Europe
Increasing numbers of women work as astronomers in universities and observatories. At the Royal Astronomical Society, women serve on the Council, and women officers include **Carole Jordan** and **Kathy Whaler**.

Glossary

Aeronautics The science and practice of navigation in the air. Men and women who are working in this area are seeking to understand how humankind and their machines can operate in the air.

Astronaut A traveler into space, male or female. "Cosmonaut," which means exactly the same, is the term used by the Soviet Union.

Aviation The art of operating airplanes, helicopters and other flying machines. Pilots work in aviation but, unlike the Wright brothers, they may not necessarily understand why a plane behaves the way it does in the air. This is explained by the science of aeronautics.

Comet A minor member of the solar system which travels around the Sun. It usually only becomes visible as it moves closer to the Sun than Jupiter. It is in this position that a comet is usually discovered.

Commercial airlines The business organizations that operate scheduled air flights around the world. Air companies such as TWA, or British Airways are examples.

Control center The name given to the center of operations for space flight.

Copernican System A system based on the idea that the sun is at the center of the solar system and the planets revolve around it. It takes its name from the Polish astronomer, Nicolaus Copernicus, who first introduced this idea in the early 16th century.

Engineer A man or woman who works in the field of engineering. This is the discipline that applies pure science to create benefits for humanity in various fields, such as mechanics, electricity and chemistry.

Mission specialist The non-pilot astronaut of the Space Shuttle. Astronauts with this role are responsible for satellite launchings, operation of the remote manipulator arm and the day-to-day in orbit "housekeeping."

NASA This stands for National Aeronautics and Space Administration. Set up in 1958, it is responsible for the American program of space exploration.

Nebulae These appear as fuzzy patches of light in the night sky. Today we know that a nebula is a cloud of gas and dust associated with certain stages in the life cycle of a star. The 18th century astronomers did not know this.

Payload bay The area located behind the cabin of the Space Shuttle where cargo, such as satellites and instrumentation, is carried.

Payload specialist A scientist who works aboard the Space Shuttle. He or she is not a regular member of the astronaut team. The payload specialist will fly in the Shuttle to operate a particular payload (i.e. cargo) on board.

Physicist Someone skilled in the science of physics, the study of all natural things. An astrophysicist works in the physics of the heavenly bodies.

Pioneers Women and men who are the first to take a course of action which is later followed by others. All three of the women in this book were pioneers. They were the first to become involved in their particular areas of the unknown.

Prejudice Prejudice is shown when someone unfairly favors or acts against another person. This may be because the other person is from another nation or race, or is another color or sex.

Remote Manipulator Arm The mechanical arm on the Space Shuttle which is used by the crew from inside the cabin. It can be used, for example, to retrieve or to repair a satellite in space. Sally Ride was one of a team of scientists who helped to develop this arm.

Solar system The Sun and the group of astronomical bodies associated with it. The main members of the solar system are the Sun and the planets Mercury, Venus, Earth, Mars, Jupiter, Saturn, Uranus, Neptune and Pluto. Minor members are comets and asteroids (minor planets).

Sweeping A term used by astronomers to describe a systematic search of the night sky. Caroline Herschel used her telescope to sweep the heavens for comets.

PLACES TO VISIT

The following organizations may be able to help with additional information.

In Britain, information sheets and a booklet by Patrick Moore have been produced by The William Herschel Society and these are available from Herschel House.
Herschel House,
19 New King Street,
Bath
which is the house where Caroline lived with her brothers William and Alexander in the late 18th century.

Mt. Wilson Observatory, Pasadena, California 91109.

National Air and Space Museum,
Smithsonian Institute
7th Street and
Independence Ave., SW
Washington, DC 20560
The Smithsonian has exhibits on technology, aeronautics and space explorations.

National Aeronautics and Space Administration (NASA)
NASA Headquarters Information, Washington D.C. 20546
NASA has field installations and space centers throughout the United States.

Index